Basic Socialism:

Why Socialism is Sexy Now

By Edward Lawrence

Basic Socialism: Why Socialism is Sexy Now
By Edward Lawrence

***ISBN:** 9781797754277*
***Imprint:** Independently published*

*Published by **We Are Socialism***

Madrid, Spain

Why is everyone talking about socialism?

In an age of political disillusionment, when all politicians seem to be carbon copies of one another, people are shunning the mainstream and looking for radical ideas. Socialism is one such idea. This book aims to explain why people are turning to socialism for answers in an increasingly turbulent world.

But what do socialists actually believe?

And what is the difference between a democratic socialist and a social democrat?

This first book in the *Basic Socialism* series explores these questions, asks what sets socialism apart from other political ideas, and discusses how it should look to its roots to help shape a brighter future.

We look at different strains of thought within socialism itself, consider why it lost its appeal, and reveal how this time-honoured progressive movement became popular again in the era of tech start-ups and Instagram.

Socialism is sexy again. Here is why.

For Daisy

Table of Contents

Acknowledgments

This book is dedicated to my friends and family, who put up with my sharing of bad memes online and constant conversations about socialism.

I would like to thank Matt Morgan and Ian Sowers for polishing and proofreading the book, as well as Tim Appleton for their valuable input and perspectives. All three have been instrumental in making it possible.

Finally, I'd like to thank my wife, Laura, for her unwavering support, and for putting up with my incessant ramblings.

Introduction

Socialism is the future

Socialism is the language of change. Its message is *hope*.

Hope for a more equal and humane society. This will not change overnight.

Socialism needs to make changes in small communities, in government and on the international stage. It means solidarity and action, thoughtful and understanding debate, and it needs to create communities of people working together towards a better future.

Capitalism has evolved into the system that we all take for granted today. Socialism is questioning that system. If you feel comfortable doing that, then welcome. We aren't going to change capitalism overnight. It's going to take several countries and several parties in government to help change the system we know today. It will take many of us fighting against the powerful capitalist interests.

Even the horrors of war, climate change and the ongoing refugee crisis cannot make the system change. Therefore we must make it change, and together create a society that wants more than money, fame and commodities.

The idea for this book is to discuss socialism in a broader sense than just economics and theory; I want to discuss what it means to be a socialist and the type of society we want to achieve. Why we call ourselves socialists.

I want to look at socialist ideas without the scare stories and over-intellectualisation that have become an unhelpful label for socialists. We need a space for people to share their understanding of what socialism is to them and their world. I have realised there is a need for this since joining the British Labour Party. I was desperate to learn from other left-wing political enthusiasts. I found them, and they helped me find out why I was a socialist. This was great and overwhelming all at the same time

We will discuss socialism in a way that is accessible to everybody and not just to bookworms or people who breathe politics. Socialism is more than just philosophers, economic systems and party politics. It's a way of building a fairer world and a more equal society. Which is why many people are drawn to socialism in the first place.

The western world is the birth place, and current host, of capitalism, moreover the current from of capitalism we have: neo-liberalism. That is why current political trends in the United Kingdom and the United States of America are discussed in this book. These countries have changed and enforced the will of capitalism on many different parts of the world. Maybe now they can start to undo the damage they have done, and steer the world in a fair and green direction towards peace.

In the first part of the book we will look at the difference between socialism and capitalism; different types of capitalism and socialism; and why a more radical form of socialism, democratic socialism, is needed today. In the second part of the book, I will delve deeper into what it means to be a socialist and what most, but not all, socialists believe. In part three, I will look at why socialism is becoming sexy again and why it wasn't so hot in the past. This is a whirlwind tour of how social democracy failed in some parts of Europe and why socialism lost its sex appeal. In part four, I will discuss becoming a socialist and some practical things that you can do if you want to follow this path.

Part 1

What is socialism?

"I should tie myself to no particular system of society other than of socialism"

– Nelson Mandela

Socialism is many things to many people. To a conservative father, it might be the rebel phase that his son goes through in his early twenties before he gets a "real job". To many others it might be those social warriors that march for everything or shout down racists online. Socialists are those hippies that never left the sixties; the guy selling badges at a protest or that girl who used to be quiet but now wears a T-shirt bearing the slogan "Eat the Rich". They are probably all socialists, but there is more to socialists than that.

Chances are you had school teachers who were socialists; the nurse who looks after your grandmother could be one, as could the guy who got thrown out of the pub the other night. Socialists are all around, and some of them don't even know it. However, once you learn what it really is and what it is not, it's easy to tell if you are a socialist or not.

Socialism has been used in many different contexts. It's been used to justify totalitarian regimes such as the USSR, China, Nazi Germany and North Korea. Many refer to these as communism or a form of socialism. They are not socialism.

They were, and are, murderous regimes that kill people who they feel are inferior. They may have started out as socialist governments in name or in terms of their economic plans, but they were far from being socialist societies. This is like saying "I'm not racist, but …". Similarly, to those who say "I am a socialist, but I want to kill people who don't agree with me," my response would be: well, that isn't socialism.

Socialism has a few basic concepts. The major one, which has been at the core of socialism from the 1900s till today, is the idea of human equality. You need to believe in this idea to be a socialist; that goes without saying. The above-mentioned regimes fail on this count.

Hitler put socialists, communists, Jews, black people, disabled people and gypsies in concentration camps. Stalin had the gulags, and China at this moment is trying to convert Muslims in a large camp not visible on Google maps. These are the things socialism is fighting against.

Then there is communism. It's best to think of communism as the misunderstood, more-extreme friend of socialism. Many say it has never been tried. Karl Marx, the Father Christmas-like philosopher of the left, never actually provided a blueprint of how communism should work. That's the problem: if no one really said how it was meant to work – But hey! That's philosophy for you! – then why do people hijack it to justify dictatorships? The answer is just that: it's a justification for something else, for a totalitarian government. If I stick a Mercedes badge on a Ford, it doesn't make it a Mercedes.

But we are here to talk about socialism and not communism. You will see the difference later.

Socialism and capitalism

Socialism is on the left of the political spectrum. The political spectrum is a way of defining somebody's political beliefs. It goes from left to right, with a bit in the middle called the centre ground. This spectrum mainly involves how people would run the economy; however, it is about much more than just who owns what and who pays the most taxes. The economy sounds boring, but it really affects more than just money and stocks and shares.

Our modern-day economy is capitalism. Capitalism is what our society is built around. It's why we work; buy houses; study for better jobs; and aim for promotion. It is the basis of why we sell the things we produce and buy things with our wages. It is a man-made concept, and many say that money is the religion of the 21st century and shopping centres are the church.

It started in the United Kingdom just before the Victorian era with the invention of the steam engine. From there it has flourished into the multinational corporations of today, such as Google, PricewaterhouseCoopers, Microsoft and Inditex. That, along with the invention of the stock market, gives us the 21st century economic system that we are all led to believe is "just how it is meant to be". Socialism challenges this line of thought.

Capitalism is the economic system that allows humans to buy and sell commodities. Owners of factories and companies run services. Offices employ workers to work for them, and they pay them for their work.

By being employed, workers produce services, products and commodities for other people to buy or utilise.

People pay a price for what is produced by the worker, and the bosses take the money and pay the worker a wage out of it. The wage is normally fixed by the owners. The worker uses that money to buy things they need to live as they don't own any means of producing things, such as factories, other than their own labour. They must sell their labour to live, hence the expression "living hand to mouth".

The owners use the money they make from selling their product for several things: investment in new technology to keep up with the competition and produce more products to make more money; maintain buildings and equipment; and paying the workers.

Whatever is left goes to the owners as surplus profit.

If the owners make cuts in wages and investment but maintains or increases productivity, then they can make more surplus profit. That means more money for the owners and less for the workers, despite their working the same or harder.

This is a basic outline of how capitalism works. This is why Karl Marx is so famous. It's what he critiqued, among other things. He went on to critique capitalism further, saying that eventually the competition between companies would mean that companies got bigger. In turn, some would eventually have to succeed, and others would fail. Today, we see companies buying up other companies and independent traders getting put out of business as they cannot compete. This isn't progression; this is capitalism.

Is capitalism bad?

It is an economic system like feudalism before it. After all, kings and queens had their uses: they funded trips to allow Europeans to conquer, and invade, the Americas, Australia, New Zealand and many other islands. They also funded artwork and inventions, such as those of Leonardo da Vinci, and beautiful castles that we can walk around nowadays when we are on holiday. However, this economic and political system of kings, lords and serfs came to an end with the emergence of democracy and international trade. Society progressed and eventually feudalism was replaced by the capitalism we see today.

Capitalism has funded research into medicine to help eradicate diseases, built weapons to defend countries, and brought many people out of poverty. However, like the kings before it, it is not perfect – and this cycle will eventually come to an end.

Marx wrote critically of capitalism in *The Communist Manifesto*, but he also wrote small tributes where he acknowledges the progress it has helped us make as a society.

Marx said "Modern industry has established the world market, for which the discovery of America paved the way. This market has given an immense development to commerce, to navigation, to communication by land." [1]

He obviously goes on to critique capitalism and argues that owners of companies will need to expand their markets to ensure they continue to make a profit. He also states that they spread all over the globe and make connections to every corner of the earth [2].

In the past 100 years, capitalism has spread to India, Africa and China, establishing the same system there as it has here in the West. Whilst it improves poverty, it also makes people become wage slaves as they have no option other than to work. Often, in developing countries, capitalists make these people work in unsafe conditions and do not invest in the equipment, staff or buildings.

This has led to many catastrophes and even deaths. In 2013, a garment factory in Bangladesh collapsed, killing 1,135 people. The workers had complained about the unsafe working conditions and the crumbling walls, but they were ignored. The five-storey building came crashing down and killed many of the people working there.

Bangladesh is the second biggest clothes exporter in the world and makes $218 billion dollars a year from exports, whilst workers are paid the equivalent of $68 dollars a month. Safety concerns were raised after the incident, but this neglect of workers continues in pockets of developing counties all over the world today, so that we in the West can have cheap T-shirts bearing capitalist logos [3].

Marx went on to predict that the more profit a company makes, the more money the owners of the companies will have and less the workers will have. Oxfam reported in 2017 that the world's eight richest men had the same wealth (£350 billion) as 50% of the world's population. They went on to claim that this is because of wage suppression, tax avoidance and companies focusing on profit for the owners. A London-based CEO earns the same as 10,000 people working in sweatshops in India for a year! [4]

Many socialists believe that capitalism has reached the end of its course and that we should begin the process of replacing it with something more humane. This is the socialist economic model, where workers are not exploited by the owners and profits are reinvested into the companies and distributed fairly between the workers. The workers own the companies as part of cooperatives, and equality is made a priority for society. Socialists differ on this topic and that will be discussed later.

Where on the spectrum are you?

Most people's political beliefs and opinions towards capitalism hover around the centre of the spectrum, with some going a little to the left or right. This is normally dependent on factors such as their financial background, upbringing, experiences, nationality and current beliefs. Many feel we have been led to believe that capitalism is the natural order of things; how life is meant to be. Is it?

The political spectrum is much like anything else. Take Harry Potter fans for instance, you get completely obsessed people who name their children after the characters down at one end, and you get people who hate Harry Potter at the other end.

OK, bad analogy! But you get the idea. On the right-hand side they love capitalism, and on the other side they don't.

Right of the centre you have conservatives, or the so-called right wing. Close to the centre, it starts out mildly pro-business and in favour of capitalism and then slowly works out towards pro-capitalists who want no government intervention in the market. This is what they mean when they say the "free market" – a market free of government intervention. That is, of course, until you have a recession like the one in 2008. Excuse my cynicism.

On the left, things get more anti-capitalist the further you go out. Towards the centre of the left you have people who want a more equal society but who believe capitalism can be tamed by the government. The further left you get, the more a person believes that the government should be involved in the market, and that the eventual replacement capitalism is a good idea. If you continue to the left, you eventually get to communism. This is the belief that all of the economy should be controlled by the government, with no room for private property or private business.

It's not all about the economy

But it's not that simple.

After you have thought about and included economic positions, which some people aren't interested in, then you start to include other aspects of people's beliefs.

These include beliefs on things such as nationalism, tradition, religion, equality, immigration, work ethic, how society should work, the welfare state, sexuality, race, gender equality, access to health care and the military. It also considers what a future society should look like – how it should be organised and what the general ethos of the society should be. The more you read and learn about these areas, the more you identify your own political beliefs. This helps you to discuss current affairs with people and analyse information when you hear it. This goes on to influence how you vote and who may get into power and run the country. That's why fake news is such an issue now: it basically sways people into voting for parties they may not agree with. The Internet has changed everything.

Some extreme beliefs have been labelled as *far right* or *far left* – as in they are on the very right or left end of the political spectrum. This is normally more about their views on society than their economics.

This may seem straightforward to many, but for others these labels can just go straight over their head. It's important to remember that people are complex, and that these labels really don't mean a lot sometimes. There are left-wing racists and right-wing homosexuals: don't always judge a person by their politics. Unless they are Nazis of course.

A person's opinions or beliefs may determine where they would be placed on the political spectrum. Unlike Harry Potter, it isn't just a case of liking or disliking capitalism.

These labels came about following the French Revolution. They were dependent on where you sat in the parliament. Those on the right of the building, near the king, were for the monarchy and tradition. Those on the left were progressive and anti-monarchy. Those in the centre were a bit of everything.

We still use these labels today as a simple guide. Yet they are not completely descriptive. Many others have been tried and not stuck. It can get overly complex at times as the meanings of labels change and mix together.

The truth is, no ideology or label is singular to a country. All these ideologies have, over time, helped form the society we live in today. Political ideologies have helped shape this world, for better or worse, along with immigration, colonisation, wars and tragedies in our own countries and in other people's. In early society, human interaction with the earth around us determined our way of life; later, this was the role of cultural and religious movements.

Now, politics and the economy help define how we live and how we treat the earth. They also determine how countries see themselves and how they treat other countries. They also guide how we treat each other.

Today, we all live in what many call a mixed economy. The mixed economy includes how people spend, exchange and earn money. It also includes the population's relationship with work, consumption of material goods, and even how we judge each other – even how materialistic we are. Capitalist and socialist features in an economy can make big differences to these factors.

Countries with more hallmarks of socialism, such as Denmark, Sweden, Norway and Finland, the Scandinavian countries, tend to be less materialistic, healthier, less violent and more empathetic. Socialist hallmarks include high-quality, free healthcare, free education, established workers' rights, a fair minimum wage, a progressive tax system, adequate maternity leave, a fair welfare state, state housing, rehabilitation rather than punishment for criminals, strong workers' unions and state-managed, well-funded infrastructure.

Countries with higher levels of financial inequality tend to have more capitalistic hallmarks. These include services provided by private companies, a small welfare state, minimal state housing, weaker workers' rights, and minimum taxation. This all leads to a capitalist society that will have higher levels of financial inequality. As I mentioned earlier, eight men own more than half the world's wealth. That alone is proof that capitalism isn't working for everyone.

Financial inequality isn't about the number of poor people in a country. It's about the difference between the number of poor and rich people. It's the difference between the haves and have-nots.

In the book *The Spirit Level* [5], the authors demonstrated that many problems in society, such as health and social care problems, are related to income inequality. These include problems such as life expectancy, maths and literacy levels, child death rates, teenage birth rates, obesity, mental health issues and levels of imprisonment, all of which are worse in countries with a bigger income gap. Income inequality refers to the difference in the wages between the highest and lowest earners and the relative size of these groups.

Countries with high rates of these problems and higher levels of income inequality include Portugal, the USA and the UK. Generally, the bigger the income gap a country has, the higher rate of problems it experiences.

The USA has some of the highest levels of financial inequality, as well as the highest levels of health and social care problems. It's also the richest economy in the world and the modern-day home of capitalism. Not quite a coincidence.

Countries with less health and social care problems are the Scandinavian countries. In the middle, those with fewer problems than the USA but more than Denmark include Ireland, Italy, Australia, France and Germany. Countries with more socialist hallmarks in their society have less income inequality and, more importantly, fewer health and social care problems such as those listed above. Wilkinson and Pickett then took their research further in a subsequent book, *The Inner level* [6]. In their latest work, they conclude that as the income gap has got bigger the rates of health and social care problems have got worse. In *The Inner Level*, the authors explore mental health in greater depth. In countries with higher levels of income inequality, people are also more prone to mental illness. The more financial inequality, the higher the rates of depression, suicide, anxiety, antidepressant prescriptions, and drug and alcohol abuse.

I certainly saw this while working as a mental health nurse in the UK. I moved from a large town in the south-west to London, where there is more financial inequality. I learned that, even if you only move down the road (well, motorway), you can see a huge difference in the incidence and severity of mental illness.

They also claim that, in countries with higher levels of income inequality, people are more concerned about how they are seen by others. Surprisingly, this is not dependent on their level of income. Poor and rich people are generally more judgemental and vein in capitalist countries.

I personally relate – and I'm sure you can too – to the constant thoughts of keeping up with everyone else, having what everyone else has, and trying to emulate celebrities. A constant feeling that your personal worth is defined by what you are wearing or where you are working. As many of us know, it's bloody exhausting.

These findings show that capitalism is not the perfect system. Countries like the Scandinavian countries and even more-moderate ones like Spain have high levels of happiness when ranked alongside other countries. Why is this? They have one factor that is common throughout: the hallmarks of socialism.

The hallmarks of socialism include things like more empathetic societies that are less judgemental, superficial and materialistic. You could say they have higher rates of socialism built into their society.

This isn't flawless. Germany and the USA have high levels of financial inequality and so does the UK. They have some hints of socialism, but they are far from perfect. Why?

This is because societies change, and they have become more capitalist over time. General progress in society has been accomplished over time through things such as free education for all, motorways, public libraries, public transport, museums, state-managed media, postal services, health and safety laws, and the welfare state (social security to Americans). It was the unions, workers, suffragettes, scientists, inventors, socialists, protestors, and soldiers that fought and battled for these things that we take for granted today.

These are all funded by taxes and are essentially socialism in practice. We must save these things and expand on them. This is one of the goals of the socialist project. Protect our countries' services and build on them.

Capitalism says it wants to improve them with free market economics. They will say this is in the name of progress, modernity or market choice. Really, it's motivated by profit. One example of this is the UK's National Health Service (NHS), which is slowly being privatised. Capitalists will make money out of anything if we let them.

Trade unions
The history of trade unions is long, and they have fought some very hard and tough battles. Trade unions are based on the idea of collective bargaining on behalf of the worker.

When you say "union" to most people, they immediately think of strikes. Then they instantly think they are after more money. Whilst this may be the case in some strikes, normally it is about far more than just money. It's about things like pressure from employers to be more productive despite health and safety concerns; lack of workers' rights, such as holiday or sick pay; or the right to renegotiate pay so that it is fairer for all. It may also be in solidarity with other workers that are striking.

Joining a union is a simple idea. We are stronger together and we can negotiate with the owners of the companies for more rights, better pay and safer working environments. Workers aren't exploited as much as they could be. In the media, you often see the unions arguing with the bosses, but most of the time unions work well with companies to help them maintain workers' satisfaction with their jobs or to represent workers when they are dealing with their employer.

Unions are the ones who got you weekends, shorter working hours, paid holiday, and fair contracts, and who will also be by your side if you ever need advice or guidance when dealing with employment issues.

Union membership has fallen as people have come to take workers' rights and employment law as a given. Unions also lost a lot of bargaining power as capitalism grew stronger. The USA and the UK both had strong unions in the 1980s until they were disassembled by Ronald Reagan and Margaret Thatcher. To read more about this time, look up "UK miners' strike" and "Reagan and the air traffic controllers' strike".

Modern-day capitalism and its inequalities

You may have heard the term neoliberalism. This started back in the late 1980s, when Reagan and Thatcher both adopted a radical economic plan. This was set out by Friedrich Hayek, an Austrian economist famous for his theories on liberal (free market) economics from the1940s right up till the 1990s. [7]. Margaret Thatcher was a famous admirer of his. Whilst waving one of his books, she once declared "This is what we believe" to a table of ministers during a meeting.

Later, Milton Freeman and other economists from the Chicago school of economics – nicknamed "the Chicago boys" – took the concept of the free market even further. They implemented their theories in late-1970s Chile under the dictatorship of General Pinochet, with the help of the CIA. They privatised the state-owned businesses and services and helped stabilise inflation. Some refer to it as the Miracle of Chile, but it caused a crash in 1982 and the government later took over control of greater sections of the economy. This time period is still a point of debate for some economists [8].

Without going into too much detail, the basic idea of neoliberalism is to expand the free market. They want to privatise and monetise public services. A good example of this is when Margaret Thatcher denationalised the railways and the gas, electricity and telephone companies. This meant that shareholders could buy into the public services and make money from the taxpayers. It was sold to the public as a way to increase choice and efficiency. Following this, there was a boom for capitalism, with more money floating around as there was more stuff to buy and sell.

This is where the idea of "trickle down" economics comes in – the idea that if people are making money at the top, then it will flow down to the bottom. This is about as believable as Santa Claus. Remember: eight men own 50% of the world's wealth.

Neoliberal capitalists also aim to minimise public spending and borrowing and help private business make profit whilst paying minimal taxes. This is where the idea of a "small government" comes from.

This initiative was continued in the USA and over much of the western world. Workers' rights were decimated and the unions lost a lot of power. This changed the whole ethos of how society is viewed and how the country runs services for its citizens.

Subsequently it led to a rise in individualism and materialistic thinking. Humans have always had a degree of ambition and competition. However, this economic system put more weight and more belief behind this. That is why many people are complaining that people are more greedy and competitive in the modern world than they were in the past. Statements such as "No one cares about each other" and "No one knows their neighbours anymore" are a sign of the secular times we live in. I personally feel you can see how competitive a society is by the amount of neoliberalism it has in

its economic system. Everything is for sale –
mental health, selfie sticks, insurance for your
goldfish. You can literally buy anything these days
and people seem more concerned about material
goods than about others' wellbeing or experiences.
Move to London and you will see what I mean.
However, apparently young people are now
investing more in experiences and travel than in
material goods. Which is a good sign that not all
hope is lost.

Individualism makes people responsible for
themselves in the eyes of society, no matter what,
and frees the state of any responsibilities it has
towards promoting equality. They put pressure on
people to take responsibility for their own futures
even if they are completely disempowered by
inequality. This includes things such as race,
gender, financial income and social class.

They really do push the message of "survival of the
fittest" and that if you have lots of money, you
probably deserve it. However, if you look at most
rich people, 60% of them in the case of the UK,

most of them have this handed down to them by their parents and their parents before them. Or they have better opportunities as a child, such as going to private school or having a private tutor, which allowed them to reach the top of the ladder faster than those who lacked those opportunities. People do have a responsibility for their actions, decisions and behaviours, but the state also has a responsibility to ensure that people have equal opportunities. If this isn't the state's job, then what is it there for?

The Sutton Trust, a foundation that helps improve social mobility in the UK, reported in 2016 that 74% of judges, 71% of barristers, 61% of doctors, 51% of journalists and 50% of the cabinet ministers had gone to private school. Only 7% of children in the UK go to private school. Also, 67% of Oscar winners and 63% of Nobel prize winners had gone to private school. [9]

By making society more competitive and less equal, this pushes the belief – and helps fixate the idea – that some human beings are worth more than others just because of their income status or because of the fact they have more followers on Instagram. Social media has cast greater light than ever on how we interact, judge, and help – or don't help – each other.

Socialism's idea is to calm this competitive, individualistic nature and to try and get people to work together for the benefit of each other and society. This does not mean making everybody a boring carbon copy of one another, but it does mean paying taxes and being more empathetic and less judgmental towards your fellow human being. Socialism does not expect people to change overnight and it isn't going to force people to change their ethics. However, by changing society slowly we can build a better world.

Countries these days are becoming more globalised and competitive. However, there are countries that are not so competitive, and it is no coincidence that they have a less neoliberal economic system. This is one big difference I have noticed in moving from the UK, which is hyper-neoliberal, to Spain. Whilst no countries are perfect, I can tell you that people here are more warm, friendly and empathetic than in the UK. I do believe this is partly to do with the different levels of socialism and capitalism in place in both countries.

Social democracy vs democratic socialism

"Democracy is the road to socialism."
– Karl Marx

Socialism branches from the centre-left, where people believe in a form of the welfare state and equality. The people whose beliefs are closer to the centre believe in humanising the capitalist economy, and if you go a bit further left, they want to eventually replace it.

It depends on the country, but people on the centre-left are normally referred to as social democrats. They try to provide good services for the public whilst trying to remain pro-business but against the exploitation of workers. Their aim is to make capitalism fairer for all by humanising it.

In some countries this has worked and in others it has been done as a way to keep people quiet; others say it has not gone far enough. In many countries, such as Sweden, they had a strong union base in their society and had a more equal society to start out with – i.e. before social democracy arrived. This allowed social democracy to flourish and work efficiently for society.

Sweden is a good example of this; they have a heavy influence of socialism in their society and workers have good representation at many different levels of the economy and in businesses. This ensures that worker exploitation is lower, whilst profits are maintained. It is not a perfect country by any means, but capitalism and social democracy have an understanding, although this is not always perfect. [10]

In other countries with less progressive social democratic parties, there has been a trend of legislating for minimal financial regulations on businesses. Depending on the regulation, this will determine if it does something. A good example of this is the minimum wage for employees, which is effective.

As we continue, we get to the point that I want to get to: democratic socialism.

Democratic socialism

Now, social democracy can work, and it overlaps with what I am about to talk about. However, my argument is that in much of Europe social democracy slowly stopped being socialist at its heart. It did this by embracing capitalism and ultimately ended up working for it. Many people are now turning to a more radical form of socialism as they feel it does challenge capitalism. This is democratic socialism.

Aneurin Bevan, a British Labour politician and architect of the NHS, said in a speech in Blackpool on 29 November 1959:

"Democratic Socialism is not a middle way between capitalism and Communism. If it were merely that, it would be doomed to failure from the start. It cannot live by borrowed vitality. Its driving power must derive from its own principles and the energy released by them. It is based on the conviction that free men can use free institutions to solve the social and economic problems of the day, if they are given the chance to do so. You cannot inject the principles of ethical Socialism into an economy based upon private greed."

Democratic socialism is more critical of capitalism than social democracy. It is further to the left on the spectrum. Social democrats believe they can humanise capitalism and maintain it, whereas democratic socialists want to change capitalism to a socialist economy via democratic means. This is gradual though. They don't want to throw CEOs from the top of skyscrapers in New York. They don't want to burn down the stock markets and steal from the rich. They just want to spread the wealth equally between people.

"From each according to his ability, to each according to his needs" is the socialist mantra. It means that everyone contributes to society what they can and take from it what they need. Essentially it is about paying taxes and using services.

Democratic socialists plan to change capitalism by advocating for cooperatives, shared ownership and good representation of workers in companies. That's only the start, but it would level the playing field for the future. They also want to stop heavy tax avoidance by businesses and ensure that public services remain services: not fruits for shareholders to squeeze dry of profits.

This is also where many social democracy and democratic socialist policies overlap in their efforts to bring about change. The differences then begin to show – the democratic socialists want to push a further.

An example of this is how the economy is run. Democratic socialists want the state to have a major influence on the market by owning key industries. Whether that is owning the state airline, mines, steel and iron works, shipbuilders, utility companies, car, train and plane factories, movie production companies, or even the lottery!

These things are traded in the market, nationally and internationally, and make a profit. The main difference is that the profit is reinvested into the state and is shared amongst the workers – not the shareholders. This is called nationalisation: taking different industries and making them work for the nation not the private individual. In this economy, private enterprise is still allowed but there are rules it must follow, such as paying taxes and complying with employment laws.

Social democracy, on the other hand, works with capitalism and varies from country to country in how it manages the market. Some countries may keep certain aspects of their industry nationalised, like Germany or Spain's national train operators, and some may sell the industries off to private companies.

Services not industry

Most socialists say that the government should provide universal, free-to-access basic services, such as healthcare, childcare, dentistry, education, state housing, and sickness and unemployment benefits. They also believe that the government should control the local services for housing, such as electricity, water, social housing and gas. This is common in countries in the north of Europe such as Denmark, Sweden, Norway and Finland.

Normally, in democratic socialist societies such as the ones mentioned above, the state also owns and maintains the transport systems and builds and maintains infrastructure such as prisons, motorways, schools, libraries and hospitals. They also employ the people that work there. This was common in the UK before Margaret Thatcher started privatising most things such as the railways and amenities.

Many other countries have many socialist public services. Parts of Germany have free university education and also has a national bank that loans money to people to help start businesses. Spain's railways and lottery are nationally owned. In the UK, the BBC is funded by the state and so is the National Health Service. EDF, the electricity company, is owned by the French state.

On the other hand, social democrats in some countries have begun to let private businesses run state services such as health, postal or transportation services. The government pays the businesses to provide these services. If they meet targets, then they make a profit. Many politicians have shares in these businesses – no surprise there!

The government uses the capitalist trick of saying it's for greater efficiency and that competition will ensure that people get more for their taxes.

However, businesses try undercutting each other when bidding to provide services. They then push their staff harder and cut corners. Running a public service as a business does not work, as the main goal is making a profit rather than delivering the service.

So, as you can see, there is a slight difference between these two types of socialism.

Radical socialism

There is a third major form of socialism. These are the people who get angry at everyone else calling themselves socialists. Radical socialism is the idea that we need to replace capitalism as soon as possible. I think it is extreme and what most people fear when you say socialism. Radical socialists want to replace capitalism completely and say that all industry should be owned by the state.

Radical socialism doesn't tolerate capitalism or private enterprise. They want people to work collectively and share the returns from selling the product, or the product itself, equally between all those who produce it. Essentially "profit" becomes a dirty word.

Often this type of socialism is used as a route to reach communism and the abolition of money. Many may argue with me here, but it has been tried before, sudden nationalisation and state regulated economy, and it has struggled. China and Russia come to mind. The Chinese economy continues to do well at this time, but this is since they have started to trade with other countries and opened their market to capitalism, although the state still owns the means of production. Russia, on the other hand, fell under the dictatorship of Stalin and never recovered.

Personally, I can see the attraction of radical socialism, but I feel that, in this day and age, the democratic erosion of capitalism is more realistic and achievable. Physical revolution would be needed to implement this type of program.

Many have ended up resorting to violence, and mass murder, to implement something similar. If you end up resorting to these methods of implementation, then are you treating each other equally? No, because you are saying that the other's life is worth less than your own. Therefore you are diverging away from one of the core aspects of socialism: equality.

Part 2

What socialists want to change

"The difference between Socialism and capitalism is not primarily a difference of technique. One cannot simply change from one system to the other as one might install a new piece of machinery in a factory, and then carry on as before, with the same people in positions of control. Obviously there is also needed a complete shift of power. New blood, new men, new ideas – in the true sense of the word, a revolution."

– George Orwell
The Lion and the Unicorn: Socialism and the English Genius

Socialists, like capitalists, can believe in many different things. They may believe in the existence of God or the existence of aliens and some may even believe that American football is better than British football.

However, there are some things that many socialists agree on and this can be whittled down to some core beliefs that separate socialism from communism, conservatism and liberalism.

Socialism, like capitalism, has advanced in its view of the world and its beliefs. Theory is advanced by discussion, and it is influenced by the environment around it.

Some socialists' views will change as people don't stick to an ideology; their opinions and beliefs are formed by experiences and the environment around them. Therefore, many socialists may have differing views on the things I'm about to discuss.

The concepts I'm going to look at in this section can be found in biographies and A-level text books. The following is a mixture, but I have used my own knowledge and opinions to flesh out what they really mean to me. These are beliefs that socialism takes for granted, and they help us ensure that socialism not only stays true to its core beliefs but also evolves beyond them as part of the modern-day world we live in.

Socialism is critical of capitalism.

This is where socialism stands apart from the two other main political ideologies: conservatism and liberalism.

The reason it stands out is because it is not wedded to capitalism. Conservatives and liberals both believe that capitalism is the best economic system we can have today. Socialists don't agree.

Now, while it may sound simple, there are many different critiques of capitalism and socialism is one of the biggest. Within socialism, there are many views of capitalism; these vary depending on the individual and whereabouts on the left they stand. [11]

People who believe in social democracy believe that capitalism can be humanised, with the government putting in regulations to stop companies exporting workers and to force them to pay more taxes. This allows the government to provide services for people, such as the welfare state, free education and free healthcare.

They feel that by doing this they are allowing the businesses to go about their work whilst at the same time providing a safe and humane existence for the companies' workers. Balancing just enough socialism and capitalism together.

These services are normally provided by the government and are paid for by taxing companies and individuals. Good examples of this can be found in the Scandinavian countries such as Denmark, Sweden, Norway and Finland, where taxes can be up to 40% of a worker's wage. Their public services are excellent because the government has the money to pay for them, and people have come to expect nothing less. Companies and rich individuals pay their fair share of taxes, as does everyone else. They have things such as free healthcare, shared parental leave and free childcare – and students are even paid to go to university.

However, recent years have seen social democracy become very watered-down in central and western Europe. Social democratic parties in Europe were at their peak in the late 1990s and early 2000s when the economy was steady and there was plenty of money to go around for businesses and state services. [10]

Many of these parties were pro-business whilst always providing services for the workers. A good example of this is Labour Party in the UK.

New Labour and Tony Blair gave the population good services whilst also being a good friend to businesses. They did this by allowing the businesses to build schools, hospitals and houses. It was basically "buy now pay later". Still, the UK had a good level of gross domestic product (GDP), a market value of good and services in a country, and it could handle the debt. It let the government provide services and the businesses make money. This was called "Third Way" economics and basically made neoliberalism work for the government and businesses. President Clinton also used this model in the USA.

This all went quite well until the 2008 crisis, which was caused by the housing bubble in the USA. Companies went bust due to ripple effects, and lots of people become unemployed and needed to claim benefits. This pushed up the deficit because people were not paying taxes, as they lost their jobs, and were also claiming benefits to be able to live. Labour got blamed for a financial crash they never caused, however some may say they enabled it.

These once-radical parties were now seen as being the same as all other politicians. And it's true. Most politicians looked the same and said the same things; they were just taking it in turns to govern. This happened in the USA, South America and Europe. People turned to the right when the left could not provide answers to the crisis.

So where have all the radicals gone?

They are here. They are democratic socialists.

They believe:

- The government should play even a bigger part in shaping capitalism and the economy.

- All services for the public should be owned by the government, and profits made from services should be used to improve services for people.

- Workers should have a stake or a say in big business.

- Universal basic services will be free to all.

- Workers should have more rights than they would have under the current economy.

- Unions will work with businesses to ensure their members get a fair deal and are treated correctly.

By giving the workers more rights, it means that they are not as heavily exploited by the companies in order to generate more profit. It also ensures that workers have a louder voice and more of a say in how the company is run.

Democratic socialists want to ensure that profit accumulated by companies, and by the government, is spread fairly between everybody in the country. This is done through fair taxation and fair wages. [10]

How the economy affects society and the people in it

As I've already pointed out, more equal and less capitalist countries have fewer problems and greater social cohesion. Socialists believe the economy plays a big part in how humans behave and how we function as a society.

This is a theory that Karl Marx is famous for. It was his belief that the economy underpins how we behave as a society and how we function as human beings. Like many socialists, he believed that capitalism makes people become more competitive and therefore greedier [12]. They become focused on their own world rather than the one around them.

This is because under capitalism you have the haves and have-nots. The haves are the ones that may own several houses or a business. Maybe they can live without working. This then gives them the advantage over people that must work to live.

The owners of the businesses are in competition with their market competitors. They must continue to make profits to ensure that they can keep up with the competition. Because of this, they lower their workers' wages and give bad contracts so that they don't have to pay as much sickness or maternity pay or taxes. (Do you see where I'm going with this? Yes, neoliberalism.)

In response to this, the workers' wages remain low and they are not able to accumulate any money.

They must spend their livelihood working to ensure that they can survive.

Eventually, with the accumulation of wealth, the haves end up with most of the money and the have-nots end up with very little. They end up finding it very difficult to make ends meet whilst others have more than they could ever possibly need. By 2020, it's predicted that 1% of the world's population will own two thirds of the world's wealth. [4]

Therefore, socialism wants to change capitalism to help scale down the gap between the haves and have nots. By doing this, they will change society and human nature itself. Therefore, a competitive and materialistic society will be replaced by a more empathetic, less commercial one.

Many socialists feel that by shrinking and restricting capitalism they will eventually be able to replace it with a socialist economic modal. This would have industry owned by the state or by workers' cooperatives. Profit would be equally distributed and reinvested into the industry.

People would have access to employment, as one of the goals is full employment. Everyone would also have the right to access education, health, housing, money and legal defence. This would end hunger, homelessness, poverty and ill health. But this will not happen overnight, and socialists know this. They know that it may take many years to replace the global capitalist system. People should not fear change: they should embrace progress.

Many people say that they "make it on their own", which is good. This is, after all, entrepreneurial spirit and the idea of the American dream. Socialists don't want them to give it all up straight away; rather, they encourage it. The more people who work and make businesses, the more jobs are created. These people then pay into society through taxes, and this helps fund services for everyone. Moreover, in a socialist economy, people would be free to innovate more as they would not have to invest their life savings into projects and would have back-up from the state. Innovation is encouraged, not stifled. If one person or group progresses, then all of society benefits; not just the people with money.

However, not all capitalists or entrepreneurs pay taxes. In the UK, for example, Google, Amazon, Starbucks and Apple have all avoided or reduced their tax payments in one way or another. This is estimated to cost the country around $500 billion a year [13] in lost taxes on profits – money that should have gone to the government for things like healthcare; to the military for better equipment; or towards building homes for homeless people or free childcare or university for the public.

We are encouraged to race against one another in this competitive society. Work, spend, earn, save and invest. People are judged by whether they have made it or not. Capitalism breeds this way of thinking and socialism helps to calm and will eventually change it.

Capitalism won't be here forever, and we must find something to replace it. Socialism can.

Real equality for all.

Going beyond mere equal opportunity, this set of beliefs advocates equal rights and the fair distribution of wealth and resources. For all.

Equality is not just about letting some poor kid from an ethnic minority family take out a loan and go to university. It is this but also so much more. It's the belief that people should be treated equally no matter what their social class, sexuality, skin colour, disability or gender. We are all human after all.

One video that went viral on the Internet really brings home the difference equality can make in someone's life; it's probably one of the most interesting things I have seen on the Internet in a long time. It's called the $100 race. [14]

Adam Donyes, a teacher, takes his class outside and asks the students to line up on a racetrack. Among the students are a variety of different people.

The teacher then tells them that they are going to race for a $100 bill. He then asks a series of questions and says if it applies to you then please take two steps forward.

The first question is "Do you have married parents?"; the second is "Do you have a father figure in the house?" The line begins to break up.

He then asks people to step forward "if you have never had to worry about your mobile phone being cut off" or if "you have never had to help your parents pay the bills" More students step forward.

Remember this is in America, where you must pay for your college/university education. He then says step forward if you didn't have to rely on athletic ability to pay for your education. Even more step forward.

Eventually he asks people to step forward if they "never had to worry about where the next meal is coming from" By this point, the students are scattered far apart.

The students are then asked to turn around. When they do, they see that many people are still on the starting line and that quite a lot of people are already near the teacher waving the $100 bill. It reminded me of kids standing in the line during physical education in school, waiting to be picked for the football team. Unfortunately, in life, you must be more than cool and good at football.

This shows how easy it is to get ahead or be left behind.

As we saw earlier, families with high incomes, and that can afford private education, are more likely to obtain better paying jobs. In recent research by Kimberley Noble, a Neuroscientist from Columbia University USA, explains that they have found correlations between family income and the cognitive ability of children. She specifically talks about children from poor income families, and about the lesser amount of grey matter around their cerebral cortex. This is the area of the brain that is often associated with heavy cognitive duties.

No, poor people are not born with a smaller brain, the reason for this is "poverty tax"- the mental strain that is put on people due to poverty- which means parents spend more time thinking and dealing with the problems and issues associated with being poor, rather than being able to spend time planning and thinking about their children. It also affects their personal relationship with their children. Noble goes on to say that recent research has shown 4,000 dollars a year extra, per family, can help improve a children's future outcomes. [15]

There have been a few videos and comments online critiquing this video and arguing that it only shows black children on the starting line. However, if you look at the clip, you can see white males and females still stood on – or near – the starting line.

Another criticism is that there are only white and black children in the video and no children of other races or disabled children. Whilst these are very valid points, that does not take away from the fact that some people have fewer barriers to overcome than others – trying to reach milestones in life is different for everyone.

People are often discriminated against for their class, background, education, gender, sexuality, disability and ethnicity. We should fight together for equality for all, no matter what our differences.

In her book *Why I'm No Longer Talking to White People About Race* [16], Reni Eddo-Lodge explains that black children in the UK are more likely to be expelled from school and less likely to be accepted to a top university. Black and Asian applicants for jobs are less likely to get an interview, and black women are more likely to have low-paid or minimum-wage care jobs than any other ethnic group. These facts, along with her descriptions of racism, show that despite the fact we have had a black president of the USA, we still have a long way to go until we have race equality.

Kristen R Ghodsee explores female inequality under capitalism in her book *Why Women Have Better Sex Under Socialism* [17]. In her studies she finds that women were more likely to stay in bad relationships due to dependence on men for income and healthcare insurance.

She compares women from East and West Germany before and after the Berlin Wall came down. She found women from communist East Germany had more confidence, were sexually satisfied, and were not easily persuaded by men and their money. However, women in West Germany were not as confident and were easily swooned by men with greater economic means.

Overall, the women from East Germany were not dependent on their husbands as they had economic independence and access to free services such as childcare and healthcare. On the other hand, women in West Germany were dependent on their husbands to provide payment for these services as women were encouraged to stay at home and not work.

Whilst times have changed for women, they are still often the partner – in a heterosexual couple – that works part-time to look after children. They may also have to take time off to look after a sick member of the family, as the caring role often falls to the women in society. They are also at a disadvantage when it comes to competing with their male peers for jobs. Women are often held to a higher standard than men and are also discriminated against because of pregnancy.

This goes to show that equality is about more than just having an equal say or chance. It's also about equal access to services and the right to be economically independent. For all.

So why shouldn't we level the playing field for those who find it difficult to even get into the race? Everyone has the right to a humane life where they shouldn't need to worry about food, a job or shelter.

As the British politician Tony Benn once said: "If we can find money to kill people, we can find money to help people."

I emphasise the need to watch this video and explore equality. Equality puts our lives and our society into context. It is not fair, and day by day the gap between the haves and have-nots is getting bigger.

Whilst the world will always have some form of haves and have-nots, surely we can close the gap and help improve everybody's quality of life – not just that of the people at the top.

Equality means being humane.

It's called common decency. Society seems to be lacking it lately.

Equality is one of most common ideals that socialists share; another is the dream to transition towards a more humane society. This goes hand in hand with equality.

Whereas many socialists may disagree on how the economy should be run or what services the government should provide, many want to transform society to ensure that social inequality and the exploitation of workers is minimal, and eventually non-existent. They want a society where people are humane to each other. [10]

A brilliant example of this comes from Bill Bryson's book *Neither Here nor There: Travels in Europe* [18], in which Bryson – an American that spent most of his adult life as a newspaper editor in the UK – explores Europe in his own way.

Arriving in Denmark, he sees a teenager on the floor who is obviously intoxicated. Bryson wonders what will happen as the crowds gather round and the police turn up. He sees the police helping the boy up and putting him in the back of their car. He enquires what will happen to him. To our authors surprise, he's told they are taking the boy home to his parents. They are not arresting him.

Bryson's reaction is vivid and warm. This really gives you an idea of the level of harmony in more socialist societies. Obviously, they are not perfect. Couples still get divorced, people get treated badly by their boss, and women still get wolf-whistled in the street, but it is a more humane society. So much so that, in 2017, *The Independent* reported that 19 Danish prisons had been closed in 2013 and five more were due to be shut down in 2017. This was due to the decline in inmates. There had been a steady decline in crime since 2004. This wasn't because everyone was nice, but more down to the approach that society had taken: rehabilitation over punishment and relaxed laws in relation to drugs [19]. As I said before, there are also lower rates of health and social care issues in Denmark, as well as higher levels of empathy and happiness. Denmark is often ranked as one of the happiest countries in the world.

Socialism means a society of solidarity and a society that shows empathy towards other humans. This is where solidarity with the working class comes in. As workers – that is, anyone who needs to work to live – we should be standing in solidarity against the people that own the companies, offices, shops and factories-.

If we don't stand together, then they will exploit us. It doesn't matter if you are black, white, gay, female, an immigrant, a refugee, old, young, or well educated, or if you left school at 14. The haves will exploit the have-nots.

By standing together, no matter who we are, we have the power of solidarity and strength in numbers. Just because you earn more than the woman that cleans your office doesn't mean you shouldn't support her. It might not affect you now, but it may in the future. Then, when they are stood by your side, you will see how much solidarity means.

Making a more humane, equal society: that is the whole point of socialism.

Part 3

Why socialism is sexy right now

"The common good is an aspiration for all of us."

Jeremy Corbyn
Leader of the Labour Party

Sexy socialism?

"Young, 'sexy socialists' are also pushing Marxism back into the student mainstream," wrote Samuel Fishwick for the *London Evening Standard* in May

2017. Yes, socialism is back on the map and it is no longer a dirty word. But when was its downfall?

Since the Second World War, there have been a few major things that have happened in the world of socialism. Following the Allied victory in the Second World War, British soldiers returned home eager for change. They didn't want to go back to how it was before the war, which was in all honesty very miserable. So, they voted for change.

Clement Attlee, a short, balding and quiet man, was standing as the Labour candidate for prime minister. He was standing against the victorious and larger-than-life statesman Winston Churchill. Following several rallies around the country from both politicians, Labour won with a landslide. Everyone was shocked that the war icon had lost.

During this government, Labour established the National Health Service, which today stands as a beacon for socialists all over the world. Universal health care had been established in the country that, 150 years earlier, gave birth to the Industrial

Revolution. Socialism was alive in the heartlands of capitalism.

Throughout Europe, social democratic parties became popular following the Second World War. Between 1945 and the early 2000s, social democratic parties would be a main feature in most countries' governments or oppositions.

In the Scandinavian countries, a form of social democracy had already been established and started changing society to be more harmonious. This is now established in their culture. However, these parties are not perfect, and some of these countries are currently going through a difficult time, as they are faced with a backlash from citizens about the amount of immigration in recent years.

In the rest of Europe, many social democratic parties established free health care and a form of welfare state. Progress swept through Europe and standards became established with the rise of the

European Union and the fall of the Soviet bloc in
Eastern Europe.

Then it lost its appeal

After making all of this progress, some social
democratic parties in Central Europe lost their way.
They became very centrist and had little to do with
socialism. Many were socialist in name, but really
they were turning towards capitalism and away
from their origins. Neoliberal capitalism was just
accepted as the norm for many politicians now.
They were just more generous than their
counterparts on the centre-right when it came to
providing for citizens.

Some believe politics moved to the centre due to
the liberal nature of the European Union, and
politics in general became very mundane. The fall
of the Soviet Union also gave socialism a bad
name. Many associated communism with socialism
and saw the failing of one as a failing of both.
Capitalism was in its heyday and became accepted
as the norm. By the late 1990s, there was little to

distinguish between left and right parties in most countries.

Politics became a career, not a chance to represent your community. Career politicians were everywhere, and many were not from working-class backgrounds. Many politicians, on both the left and the right, had backgrounds as lawyers, bankers or advisors to older politicians – hardly representative of the general population. Distrust of politicians grew, and even more so after the 2008 financial crash and a series of corruption scandals involving politicians all over the world.

One example of this is New Labour. In the United Kingdom, a charismatic and young Tony Blair won the leadership contest. He promised the Labour Party that they would win elections by moving from the left to the centre ground and by being pro-capitalist. In what was known as the "Clause Four Moment" They ditched one of their founding objectives, which was to nationalise services for the workers.

New Labour did implement many good initiatives in the United Kingdom from 1997 until 2010. During this time, they brought in a minimum wage and better rights for minorities. They built many new hospitals and schools, and they also built Sure Start Children's Centres in every city throughout the United Kingdom to help support families. Many Labour supporters felt that, in the 13 years they were in power, they could have accomplished more. Margaret Thatcher changed the make-up of society with neoliberalism. New Labour carried on this legacy. Indeed, the Iron Lady herself was once quoted as saying New Labour was her greatest accomplishment.

They did a lot of it in the interests of their capitalist friends and businesses. As I mentioned earlier, a scheme called the private finance initiative (PFI) basically turned the services over to private companies.

It allowed private companies to build schools, prisons and hospitals, and the country simply put them on the credit card. Some contracts were made exclusive, so that the companies that built the building had exclusive rights to its maintenance for the next 15 to 25 years. This meant they could charge the NHS £466 to change a lightbulb or £8,450 to install a dishwasher. [20]

PFI became an everyday word in British politics, and every town or city has some form of PFI building. They're there as a daily reminder to voters that the government handed over taxpayers' money to businesses. Between 2011 and 2017, private companies made £821 million from the NHS, all whilst it was having to save money due to the austerity imposed by the current Conservative government. That's money that could have been spent on patients. [21]

No one really gave it a second glance until everything fell apart with the 2008 finical crash. Since then, it has been a thorn in the side of the Labour Party.

However, there's a difference between borrowing to pay for things the country needs and letting capitalists make profits from it – which is what New Labour did – on the one hand and borrowing to invest in the country on the other. If you invest in the country, like many socialists want to do, then the country and its people reap the rewards of this investment. Not the capitalists. That's the difference between Tony Blair's New Labour and Jeremy Corbyn's Labour Party of today.

New Labour also turned the health and social care system into a business. All hospitals became part of an NHS trust. They were given a strict budget, had to appoint a CEO, and were expected to meet targets. This was done under the guise of modernisation and efficiency. It was really a way to privatise departments, by letting private companies bid to run services, and to make them operate more like a factory. Examples of this can be found all over the UK.

The health and social care services are now run like businesses, not like life-saving services. Suddenly, you have nurses with 20 years' experience trying to balance budgets on the wards and choose a supplier for their bandage orders.

The financial box-tickers and people with titles like "efficiency manager" and "service manager" now make the decisions. They set the targets, write the reports and make boring PowerPoint presentations. You know the ones I mean. All whilst earning more than junior doctors and nurses.

Some NHS services are put out to tender. The people that run the NHS in that area allow private businesses, not-for-profit organisations and the NHS trust (yes, they have to bid against themselves) to bid to run a service for five years. They give an estimate and a summary of how they will run the service. The people in charge of the NHS then choose a provider – normally the cheapest one, as they have savings to make due to government austerity. The cheapest is often a private business that must make a profit, unlike the other two. As we discussed earlier, if private companies want to make a profit, they need to lower standards and pay for workers and increase productivity. Then, eventually, services begin to suffer.

Virgin Care, owned by billionaire Richard Branson, managed to win £1 billion worth of contracts in 2016 and 2017. From 2013 to 2017, the number of contracts out to tender increased from 75 to 386. It's slowly eating away at the NHS. Capitalism is literally eating away socialist healthcare in the UK. Oh yes, and Virgin Care don't pay any tax in the UK. [22].

It doesn't work either. *The Guardian* reported that Virgin have had to apologise to staff in Bath and North Somerset as letters were not sent out, patients' appointments were cancelled, and staff were told to "hold off" reporting any safety concerns to the health watchdog [23]. This is just one of a whole catalogue of errors made by private companies in the NHS. This is what happens when you embrace capitalism and don't question it. Just as New Labour did.

You could apply this model to any area of government: prisons, ambulance services, the complaints phone line of the BBC, or the people who carry out fitness-to-work assessments of benefit claimants. Private companies are given targets by the government, and if they don't meet them, they lose money. We all know capitalists don't like losing money, so they will do anything to reach the targets. Even if that means not providing a good service, as happened with train services in the UK or when Carillion, one of the big PFI contractors, went bankrupt in 2018 and had to be bailed out by the government.

Another example is the PSOE, the centre-left party in Spain. Around the time of the 2008 financial crisis, the party refused to admit there was a crisis going on. By the time they acknowledged that something was wrong, it was too late. They had already lost voters' support.

This was once one of the main parties along with the right-wing People's Party, which would often win 30–40% of the vote. Since 2011, it has dropped from 43% to around 23% in 2019 [24]. This is also due to the corruption scandals that were rife across Southern Europe during the 2000s, the financial crisis, austerity and politics generally losing touch with people.

This is a familiar picture for social democratic parties across Europe, and they are now ghosts of their former selves. When they come up against more radical left- and right-wing parties, their vote share plummets. Many say this is because of their turn to the centre and acceptance of free-market capitalism as the norm. In a sense they became less radical: they became part of the system they were meant to be fighting.

The meaning of the word socialism lost its meaning in Europe.

Socialism in the USA

Over the other side of the Atlantic, America was playing war games with the USSR.

Throughout the 1950s and 1960s, the USA and the USSR were stuck in a cycle of "mine is bigger than yours". Capitalism vs communism was the main event.

Initially, there was the Korean war. North Korea, supported by the USSR and China, invaded South Korea, which was supported by the USA and other UN countries. This went on for three years between 1950 and 1953.

Then there was the start of the Cold War, which was essentially a nuclear arms race. Both sides prepared to use nuclear weapons against the other, whilst spies from both sides were rushing around trying to outdo each other. This came to a head when the Russians planned to install nuclear missiles on the island of Cuba. It was a tense time for the USA.

Several proxy wars continued to rage, with the CIA and the Kremlin pulling strings in the background. The most famous of these conflicts was the Vietnam War, which was the subject of protest songs by the likes of John Lennon and Bob Dylan. Russia backed the Vietnamese, who sent the Americans back home after a long, gory war.

There was also the fight of commodities and technology. The Russians were the first to put a man in space, but the Americans were the first to put a man on the moon. Many Americans were also shown that they led a better life than most in the USSR due to the successes of capitalism and failings of communism.

During this time, the US government engaged in a powerful propaganda drive against anybody who was a sympathiser with left-wing ideologies. Socialism was lumped together with communism and branded a failure. No one considered the socialist policies in Northern and Central Europe. Socialists were persecuted along with communists.

Even until fairly recently, anyone calling themselves a socialist was judged by people who didn't know the difference. Even today, Fox News continuously compares socialists to the likes of Joseph Stalin when this could not be further from the truth.

I mean, why is free healthcare so scary anyway?

Socialism Today

Born in the USA

I swear that, in the Declaration of Independence, it says that all men are created equal. Surely that would make it the perfect country for socialism? Well, it has a chequered past, but maybe the future will be brighter.

Being a socialist cannot be easy in the United States of America. However, one young woman, Alexandria Ocasio-Cortez, from the Bronx in New York City, redefined this label in 2018 when she became the Democratic representative in the U.S house from the 14th district of New York State.

She had to stand against 19-year incumbent Joe Crawley to run as the candidate for the 2018 midterm elections. Crawley had not been challenged since 2004, and Ocasio-Cortez had to stand against a man who represented the US establishment. [25]

Crawley spent $3.4 million fighting off the contender for his seat in the US Congress. Ocasio-Cortez spent just under $200,000 on her grassroots campaign, starting off her online campaign video by saying "women like me are not meant to stand for seats like this". With a mix of savvy media hipsters, social networking, passion and an appeal to voters, she had the edge [26].

The self-styled democratic socialist related to the people easily with her opinions on how the system should work for everyone and her vocal support for change. The fact that she was only 29 and still working as a barmaid probably gave her some extra clout with the crowds. She took this position despite growing up in a middle-class white environment and studying politics at Boston University. Yet her speeches were full of empathetic messages that resonated with what the people were thinking: Why are we struggling to make ends meet in one of the richest countries in the world?

Following her win over Crawley, she was barraged by the media, who were instantly taken with the fact that she was using the label democratic socialist. News channels of all types were explaining, in their own way, what a democratic socialist was.

With her new fame and attention, she won the November 2018 midterms with 78% of the vote in her district. In any case, this district was a safe Democrat seat. They have had two Republicans in almost 100 years.

During the midterm elections, the Democrats won back control of the House of Representatives. Among the new representatives were the first two

Muslim women to sit in the United States Congress. One of these women, Rashida Tlaib, also identified as a democratic socialist. She had the backing from the Democratic Socialists of America, which is a socialist activist group that campaigns to elect socialists in the Democratic Party. After Tlaib was inducted as a congresswoman, she vowed to "impeach the motherfucker!'" in reference to Donald Trump. [27]

Socialism is nothing new in the United States. It has a long history of workers' unions that stretches back to the founding of the Industrial Workers of the World in Chicago. However, since the Cold War with Russia, the Left has been hard to find in the States.

During the run-up to the 2016 election, the Democrats made a mistake. Bernie Sanders, a long-term democratic socialist who normally stands as an independent, ran against Hillary Clinton for the Democratic presidential nomination.

Despite widespread support, the party chose Hillary Clinton, a well-known member of the establishment and former First Lady, to run against the no-holds-barred renegade, anti-establishment capitalist Donald Trump. Trump stood on a platform of being anti-establishment and Clinton was an example of this.

We all know what happened next.

Bernie Sanders is now 77 years of age, and he has announced that he will stand as the Democratic candidate in the next election. Sanders raised over 5.9 million dollars within 24 hours of announcing his presidential candidacy for the 2020 elections. [28]

So, will we ever see a socialist in the White House? At this moment in time it's possible.

Since Ocasio-Cortez has been nominated and been taking Congress by storm all documented on her Instagram account, the Democratic Socialists of America's membership has soared!

Sanders made socialism acceptable again in 2016 when he ran for the Democratic nomination, and Ocasio-Cortez has made it main stream. Now it is up to Sanders to make America, not just great again, but the greatest again.

According to one poll, from 2018, the future looks brighter for socialism now that the youth are not tainted with the Cold War hysteria of "reds under the bed". Gallup [29] polled 1,505 people at random and found that 51% of surveyed 18–29-year-olds had a positive opinion of socialism, with only 45% feeling positively about capitalism. Overall, Americans still prefer capitalism to socialism, but the results in the younger part of the research look positive.

So, there is hope yet… That is, if the United States can ever throw off their paranoia surrounding socialism.

Great Britain. The United Kingdom. Ole Blighty.

"Oh, Je-re-my Cor-byn!"

These were the words chanted by a crowd at Glastonbury Festival to the tune of The White Stripes' *Seven Nation Army*.

(Yes, this really happened.)

Jeremy Corbyn has a lot in common with Bernie Sanders. They are both older gentlemen with grey hair. Both identify as socialists and both have been in politics for almost 40 years. Before now, no one was that bothered by two old leftie politicians. Now, the establishment is petrified.

Jeremy Corbyn has been the Member of Parliament (MP) for Islington North, a multicultural area of north London, since 1983.

In Britain, the leader of a political party is nominated by its members, who pay a yearly fee to vote within the party and help debate policy. The Labour Party doesn't have hordes of millionaires plying them with cash. When a person is elected as leader, they remain in the post for as long as they have support.

In 2015, the party was lost in a sea of plastic, distrusted politicians. After 13 years in power, losing two elections, one disastrous war, a financial crash and failed privatisation projects, Labour was struggling in the polls and losing votes.

Many working-class people left the party as soon as they realised Labour was no longer truly socialist or for the working class. There was a huge exodus at around the time of the Iraq War.

On a whim, Jeremy Corbyn was added to the leadership ballot in 2015. This was called following the resignation of Ed Miliband after Labour had lost their second general election in a row. This time, they lost even more seats than in 2010.

There were three candidates prior to Corbyn's nomination being announced: Yvette Cooper, Liz Kendall and Andy Burnham. They did not see Corbyn as a threat at first. All three had similar politics – watered-down social democracy – and were pro-austerity. Many thought a woman would win, as Labour was light on female leaders. Andy Burnham was the favourite as he was the more left-wing candidate. "Soft left" they referred to it as, with no mention of the word socialism.

Yet all three were sticking by austerity that the incumbent Conservative Party were deepening on the back of their new majority in parliament. This is where Corbyn came in. After barely scraping enough nominations from MPs to get on the ballot, Corbyn obviously stood out. He was the only one who stood on a completely different platform. The others were like plastic moulds of politicians; Corbyn, with his ill-fitting suit and gentle but quiet manner came across as something different.

Many Labour members that left during the move to the right, under Blair, were now coming back. Under Ed Miliband, changes were also made to the rules for voting in the leadership contest. "Supporters" of Labours goals could register to vote for just £3.

After touring the country and packing out several meetings, Corbyn won with the biggest majority in any leadership election in the history of the Labour Party, outstripping his closest contender by over 40% after two rounds. Even the large number of non-members who had paid £3 to become "registered supporters" didn't make a lot of difference. Corbyn won more votes than Tony Blair had done in 1994.

The newly enthused membership created a group within the Labour Party called Momentum. This young and pragmatic group transformed the party and gave it a new lease of life. They are supportive of Jeremy Corbyn and in touch with the youth of today. They brought change to the Labour Party and have given it the upper hand over the Tories.

They are media savvy and one step ahead when it comes to campaigning for change. They run political education groups and hold positive forum meetings, get involved in local causes, and attend protests nationally. They are essentially the youth club for the Labour Party.

Momentum are disliked by the right of the party and are smeared by the press as Trotskyite infiltrators. However, they are just young enthusiastic people who want to campaign for a Labour government and bring about change in this capitalist creation we currently inhabit.

Corbyn becoming leader of the party upset a lot of people too. In the few years following the leadership election, there were two coup attempts and a leadership challenge against Corbyn. The hangers-on from New Labour, the Blairites, were not happy that their party was about to move to the left and away from their capitalist-supporting establishment. The democratic socialists had power and they had the support of the membership too.

First came a vote of no confidence in June 2016, in the aftermath of the EU referendum. This followed the mass resignation of 38 MPs, most were in shadow cabinet positions. A vote of no confidence was passed with 172 votes to 40. Corbyn, though heavily outnumbered in the parliamentary party, knew he had the support of the membership and trudged on as leader.

Despite this, he was challenged for the leadership, first by Angela Eagle and later by Owen Smith. Initially, the right of the party tried to keep Corbyn off the ballot paper for the leadership contest. However, the National Executive Committee (NEC) of the Labour Party announced that Corbyn would automatically be on the ballot as the defending leader. However, many new members and supporters were denied the right to vote unless they paid a fee of £25. Many paid up to vote for Corbyn. [30]

Smith tried to hold a rally, at which he shamefully gave away free ice creams to woo supporters. But that didn't seem to work, as the rally was half empty. On the other side of the race, Corbyn had people queuing from the early hours of the morning; it was as if a rock star had come to town. Corbyn then increased his majority by two percentage points in the leadership contest. [31]

2017 elections

Theresa May took over as prime minister following David Cameron's resignation in the aftermath of the EU referendum, which the government lost as they backed Remain. This left Theresa May with the job that no one wanted: negotiating Britain's exit from the EU. She thought she could increase her political mandate by calling a general election in June 2017.

During an election, the media are subject to different rules. Media groups such as the BBC, ITV and Sky cannot be biased during an election; they have to dedicate an equal amount of airtime to all parties and remain impartial. This does not apply to the newspapers, which – as I'm sure you are aware – are dying out anyway.

This rule meant that Jeremy Corbyn, who had been subjected to an unusually large amount of negative press, was getting more airtime and more positive coverage. By this time, I was a full convert to Corbynism.

He went on to speak at the world-famous Glastonbury festival and held mass rallies all over the country. Theresa May, on the other hand, was dying on TV.

The media gives the impression that Corbyn is not liked by many in the UK. Why isn't he popular with big businesses or the press barons? Because he wants them and their friends to pay taxes. The Daily Mail ran 17 pages of anti-Corbyn material the day before the election (yes, 17), yet Theresa May's campaign was so full of mistakes that it did her party no favours in the election.

She made a huge U-turn on the "dementia tax", a scheme where people would effectively sell their homes to fund their care when they are older. She also refused to attend televised debates, which had become a thing since 2010.

Labour went on to gain the biggest rise in its vote share since 1945. This came after the disastrous performance in 2015. Many felt Corbyn would lose even more seats, but he actually gained seats and deprived the Conservatives of their majority. They had to beg the Democratic Unionist Party (DUP), a right-wing Christian unionist party in Northern Ireland, to help form a government as they would never have had enough votes to pass laws on their own. [30]

Since then, Corbyn and the Labour Party's socialist project has gone from strength to strength. The party now has the largest number of members in Western Europe and this continues to grow.

Nevertheless, the democratic socialists in the party need to fight the media daily. Those on the right of the party, and the Conservatives, continue to try and undermine the party and anyone supportive of its leader. Scandals arise on a weekly basis and many people in Britain are starting to see that there is something about Corbyn and the newly reenergised Labour Party that the elites don't like.

The British public are walking into a neoliberal abyss where we will become subjects of our own invention: capitalism. Hopefully we will not fulfil Marx's prophecy:

"The English have all the material requisites for the revolution. What they lack is the spirit of generalization and revolutionary ardour."

Part of this message rings true: we do have the means not only to revolutionise our own country, but also to set an example for other capitalist societies. Britain is not the country it once was; it lost its empire after the Second World War and has lost its reputation for pragmatism since Brexit. A social revolution is the only way that Britain can be saved from itself. Voting Labour is a first step in the right direction, as they are the only political party adopting a different approach. The right one.

Hopefully, the socialist drive in Britain will maintain its momentum and change the materialistic nature of society that currently holds it to ransom. But even if a newly elected Labour Party does overcome the huge chasm that is Brexit, it will certainly have a fight on its hands with the establishment, the liberal and political elites, the banks, the media and the rising far right.

Part 4

Becoming a socialist

"Nothing is worth doing unless the consequences may be serious."

– George Bernard Shaw

For some time now, I've been reading and trying to understand and get involved in left-wing politics. Throughout this journey, I have come to realise that intellectual discourse regarding political philosophy is not a strong point of mine. I do, however, enjoy discussing practical and human politics, political situations that affect people: inequality, austerity, equal rights and opportunity, current affairs, and the need for a fair and rational society.

Rummaging through some brilliant – as well as some awful – books, I found this was not enough. I needed to discuss issues with people and do a little bit of soul-searching. Many people don't really know what they believe, or why they believe it, until they really explore their opinions. By doing this, I have found out key things about myself.

I am a democratic socialist.

I am from a town in the south-west of England that thrived on industry. I was taught to hate Margaret Thatcher but never really knew why. I was told: "She shut down the bloody railways; I wouldn't piss on her if she were on fire."

I then worked in the NHS for 10 years and trained as a mental health nurse. I was always interested in politics but never enough to really care unless it affected me directly. My first protest was in my home town when they tried to alter nurses' pensions. It was fun, but I was a bit lost and wasn't sure about politicians.

In 2010, I voted for the Liberal Democrats (I know, I'm sorry but it was Cleggmania) and they went back on their word of supporting the students. They propped up a Conservative government that was imposing austerity measures on the UK and raised student fees from £3,000 to £9,000 a year. Thankfully, I had finished my nurse training, but I was seeing the effects of austerity and benefits sanctions on patients in the emergency department. This was endless and made me feel very despondent about my job and politics.

After moving to London, I gained a minor interest in the Labour party leadership election. I followed Jeremy Corbyn from afar, watching him be unfairly mocked. However, I had other things to concentrate on, such as getting married and moving to Spain.

Whilst on my honeymoon, I read a number of history books, but it wasn't until I read about Spain's shady past that I took a real interest in politics. I realised I was pro-democracy and anti-totalitarian. This was cemented by my interest in Spain's dictatorship and how badly it managed its own history following the death of the dictator Francisco Franco. I just carried on from there.

I have explored both the left and the right of the political spectrum, just to make sure I wasn't a liberal or conservative. And, to be honest, I was liberally minded at the outset: accepting of capitalism and the establishment, thinking the world wasn't "that bad", and ignoring the bigger picture. Then I delved deeper. I did this by reading quite a few books, skimming articles, and watching YouTube videos. It's been interesting as I've learnt about everything from the development of human society to the changes facing the working and middle classes, as well as more specific ideas surrounding gender and race.

Was it worth it? Yes, but the best way of finding things out was – and still is – by talking to others. Asking them to explain things, their opinion, their attitudes. It all helps. Hearing people's stories, views, niche perspectives and thoughts on different subjects helps you challenge your own ideas and form new opinions. This can teach you more than any book or Facebook page.

I believe in standing up to totalitarian states and the pursuit of democratic revolution. My view is that we need to change society and the market in a democratic and peaceful way.

Socialism was a path I had already been following morally. I just didn't know it. As I said at the start, there's more to socialism than party politics and the economy. It's a way of seeing the world and the people in it.

I enjoyed helping people and saw many differences between people whilst respecting that we are all the same in a sense. Reflecting on where I come from and what I believe, I have realised that I am a product of neoliberal capitalism. I held prejudices, and still do, about people from other countries and backgrounds. Socialism has allowed me to challenge these ideas and has given me a different perspective on other people as individuals; on society, both internationally and in my own country; and on my own personal identity.

Being open to other ideologies such as anarchism and communism is something I admire. And yet I do not subscribe to these sets of beliefs. The text and theory of these movements are interesting but too utopian in my opinion. This is something I struggle with, as I feel I'm more of a practical person. Democratic socialism appeals to me because of this.

I have never aspired to be an intellectual, nor could I be one, and I come from a background which would dictate that I should be less worried about the failings of Marx and more concerned with practical matters. After all, I'm a nurse and you have to be practical. What I'm trying to say is that politics, and even more so socialism, needs all sorts of people. Everyone can have a place and, more importantly, a say.

Join the party

Ok, so this proves anyone can do it.

In December 2017, I went to my first Labour Party event. I joined the Labour Party in the summer of 2017 whilst in my home town in the south-west of the UK. The only difference to me and thousands of other people was that my first Labour meeting wasn't in my home town; nor was it in a university or in London, where I had previously lived. It was in Spain's capital, Madrid.

Prior to my first meeting, I had lived in Madrid for a year. I had searched for something to do but couldn't find much more than language exchanges or networking lunches.

During my first summer back in Britain, working as a substitute nurse to retain my registration, I became angry at the state of the NHS and decided to join the Labour Party. Previously, whilst living in London, I had been sceptical of Jeremy Corbyn and previously voted for the Liberal Democrats.

I have a clear memory of sitting in the dark, tourist-riddled pub opposite Big Ben chatting with a friend at around the time of the first leadership election. I remember not knowing who to support but thinking that Corbyn looked unelectable. I'm glad to say that, in the coming years, I was proven wrong and became an admirer of Jeremy Corbyn.

I returned to Madrid after summer and followed the Labour Party from afar. I was signed up to my Constituency Labour Party (CLP) back in Britain. I knew nothing of Labour supporters abroad. After spending several months just reading the news, I decided to google Labour supporters in Madrid. I was pleasantly surprised to come across the international wing of the Labour Party: Labour International.

Labour International is a constituency party within the Labour Party. The only difference is that it doesn't have an MP and covers members who live anywhere outside the UK. Originally it was more of a social club but, since the boom in membership across the Party, it too has gained many new members. Its membership now stands at roughly 3,600 members, who are scattered all over the world. Labour International also has the right to send delegates to the Labour Party Conference, as well as to submit motions on party policy.

I found many Labour International pages on Facebook, with a whole community of people coming together to discuss Labour Party policy. These included members from various countries around the world and from both the right and left wings of the party.

After contacting a few people, I went to a small gathering of around seven Labour Party supporters. This was in a typical no-frills bar, where we perched on low stools and talked about why we joined Labour. We came to the consensus that we would like to build a branch if we had enough people. A branch is a small group of people in a geographical area that are all members of the same party.

After my first meeting in December, I attended the next Labour Party meeting. This time, we had around 11 participants. Most people were concerned about Brexit, but many just wanted to get involved with politics in Britain. There was a wide range of people with different views and intentions.

I was unsure if I would become frustrated with the limitations of how much you can do from a foreign country for a political party. However, we have persisted. Meeting like-minded people to discuss and debate the state of politics both in Spain and in Britain has been a great success. It really makes you expand your views on everything from philosophy to voting rights.

Forming the branch also provided a focal point for Labour supporters abroad and an opportunity to socialise, discuss political issues in Britain, and become politically active. It helped me work out what I believe in and cement in my own head that I was a democratic socialist. We also enjoy another great British pastime: a beer and criticising the Tories.

You can see it is relatively easy to get involved and there are plenty of reasons to do so. Even for someone like me who lives abroad.

How to be a socialist

Do you agree with the core ideas of socialism?
Yes? Then carry on.

Now, I can only offer my own point of view, but it's
still very fresh in my mind. Here goes.

The educational stuff

Learn about your passion
As I've said, everyone is welcome – but be willing
to learn. There is loads to take in and it can feel
overwhelming. Just hang tight.

That said, everyone has an area they will be more
interested in. Whether that is internal party politics,
the environment, animal cruelty, LGBT rights,
domestic or international policy, healthcare,
immigration, fighting fascism, or philosophy.
Everyone has an area that they know something
about it.

Choose an area that interests you and read up on it; talk to others about it and even join a local group where you can learn from others. Do this and you will boost your confidence and meet like-minded people.

Learn about current affairs and ongoing issues
Even if you haven't found something that fuels your inner fire, you should at least know about a few things that have been going on. You will be surprised how often things come up that started 20 years ago.

Ongoing disputes and current events are key. Palestine and Israel, the situation in the Middle East, the EU, Russia and Putin, what's happening with China and Africa, or why the Right is growing in South America. These things can be explained in a short time by watching YouTube videos or from our good friend Google.

Find a reputable news source
When you have most of the above things down, find a good news source that will give you balanced

news reporting. Reuters is a good place to start. You can also look at more left- and right-wing news sources to see different opinions on wide-ranging situations that you may not agree with at all. Which is a good thing.

Theory
You may like to look at some theories of socialism or left-related thinking. Karl Marx is an obvious choice and the Communist Manifesto is the second most influential book in the world, the first being the bible. It's worth a read (not the bible). I'll recommend some books at the end of this part.

However, if you don't want to read, you can watch some theory on YouTube, go to political education workshops, or just learn from other people.

The practical stuff

I would encourage you to join your local political party. Before jumping right in, read some manifestos. These are a list of their policies and their beliefs. Just because a party has "socialist" in its name doesn't mean it actually is. Read several parties' manifestos before deciding if you want to join one. Remember: you can always change party later if you don't like the direction it's going in. Once you are a party member, find out where your local branch is and go along. If you need to contact someone, the secretary is probably your best bet.

If you go along to meetings, take a friend the first time as it can be nerve-racking! Don't feel intimidated by people who have been there for years or who know lots about history. Your opinion is worth just as much as theirs. It's often quite strange joining a party. They need new people to help them campaign and to keep the groups going, but some also feel threatened. Try not to worry and just go with the flow.

If you like the party or group, you may want to learn about their history. Warts and all. It's important because if you want to campaign on people's doorsteps or talk at meetings, then you may need to know a few of the basics.

Go to meetings and workshops as often as you can. Often there will be quiz nights, a programme of political education, and maybe even the opportunity to canvass. If you have a skill or aren't bothered what you do, then offer your services. I'm sure they will be very grateful!

There are more than just parties

Going to protests isn't always for everyone and they don't always have to be huge. Small protests are just as important and showing solidarity with fellow working-class people should always be encouraged.

You should also join the local branch of your professional or trade union. This is an organisation to get involved with if you are more concerned about your workplace or profession. Often, they have close links to left-wing parties and do similar activities, such as attending groups and protests. This is true class solidarity.

The other stuff

Being a socialist means a lot more than joining a political party and reading Karl Marx. Many people feel that it changes their views and opinions on life.

You might change your way of looking at things. Instead of getting annoyed about traffic jams or that there are fewer trains, you might start to show solidarity with other workers. If you see someone having a hard time or being bullied or exploited, then try and help them. I don't recommend punching your boss in the face, but see if there is anything you can do to help.

Many people become more open and accepting of other people's struggles and of people in difficult situations, such as refugees, immigrants, prisoners and sex workers. Supporting other people's choices that you don't agree with can be strange at first, but you soon see that we're all fighting some sort of battle and that a little solidarity can go a long way.

That said, just because someone doesn't agree with you doesn't mean they are wrong – just that they see things differently to you. This can be for a whole range of reasons. However, don't tolerate idiots. I'm sure you know who I mean.

Future socialism

In July 2017, the Carbon Majors Report was released, which highlighted that the top 100 companies in the world were responsible for 71% of carbon emissions. This is seriously damaging to the welfare of the planet and is causing climate change [32]. This is often uncharted territory for many, but we must unite with environmentalists – and other pressure groups – to take on yet another threat posed by capitalism. Encouraging recycling and banning fracking is only the tip of the ever-melting iceberg.

Taking account of this, and of the economic catastrophe that neoliberalism has brought upon this world, socialists must dig deep and go back to their roots as utopian visionaries. We need to give people hope and prove that a better future is possible. We must embrace green technology, switch to green energy and create green jobs. This will benefit not only the planet but also our own future and economy – and give people secure, meaningful jobs for the future. Politicians are encouraging the people to do all they can with regard to recycling, but politicians must take on the responsibility of doing something about the environment. They must hold capitalism to account. Multinational corporations are happy to derive profits from this world, but that imposes a collective responsibility on them – just like the rest of us – to deal with this oncoming storm.

"Just stop talking about philanthropy and start talking about taxes. … We can invite Bono once more, but we've got to be talking about taxes. That's it. Taxes, taxes, taxes. All the rest is bullshit in my opinion," proclaimed Rutger Bregman. The Dutch historian and writer was speaking to a room full of billionaires at the 2019 Annual Meeting of the World Economic Forum – better known as Davos – high in the Swiss mountains. [33]

Let's be honest, philanthropy and charitable donations are not enough. They have never been enough; they merely provide a passing feel-good factor for the comfortably off. We must go further as a society; we must change the economic lives of all. We must rein in the free market and no-holds-barred capitalists who think they can buy their way out. We must impose restrictions and regulations on capitalism. We must set taxes and environmental targets. The time for playing nice is over – the social democrats had their chance and failed. Now it is the turn of the democratic socialists.

Climate change is a looming disaster that will affect us all, and the current economic climate is a disaster that is affecting us all right now. The future looks bleak. We must instil hope: we must be the thinkers, the doers and the leaders of the future.

That includes embracing bold ideas to change the stagnant, unequal society that we have today. These include ideas such as a four-day working week for the same pay. Why should people work fifty hours a week with no time for themselves? They need time with friends and family, time to relax, and time to enjoy life. This is a human right. [34]

Furthermore, this can be achieved through the automation of work using robots. Work that puts human lives at risk will be done by robots in the future, but only if we make this happen. We control our future in this respect. We must get machines to work for us, to make our lives easier, rather than letting companies use them to manage us. The micromanaging of productivity, down to monitoring toilet breaks, happens and is inhuman. No one should have to work in these conditions for minimal pay. Robots can improve our working conditions rather than making them worse.
[35]

Free money? A universal basic income is the idea that everybody can have a basic standard of living and a basic wage to live on. It's been researched for years, with positive results, and is not a benefit but a right. A right that says no one should live below the poverty line. [36]Universal basic services are a step before this and make sure that no one is left without help when they need it. Basic free healthcare, public transportation, education for life, and social care if you need it. [34]

A hundred years ago, people were sceptical of free healthcare. Now it represents the standard the world over. Let's raise those standards again. We are the people who can make the future happen.

21st-century socialism

It's you; it is all of us. We are the left. We are socialism.

Socialism, like capitalism, is bigger than just the economy. It dictates how we live and what sort of society we want. Socialism is not just capitalism turned upside down; it is, and must be, about more than politics and economics. Socialism needs to change society and become part of it.

Capitalism works from the top down, and socialism must work from the bottom up. All over the world, there are people working to make the world a better place. Some protest against injustice and question the establishment, while others volunteer and help bridge gaps: these are the people who can lead and set an example for the kind of society we want both now and in the future. These people are the embodiment of socialism.

Socialism must reach into the heart of society to help tap into humanity's potential and reveal its better qualities. We must replace society's capitalist ills with a constructive and empathetic human society. We can do this by working with real people in the real world to bring about change, whether it is big or small. Change will not happen in our favour unless we work and fight for it. Most of all, we need to include everyone in this vision – no matter their class, gender, race or nationality.

We need to change the state's structure so that it is fair and equal for all, not only for those with resources or money. We must modernise and democratise our institutions and reform the government to work for the people not the market. Governments should fear the people that vote for them; that is why democracy was created in the first place. The word comes from Greek and literally means "rule by the people". We should govern the state – not be governed by it.

As well as the state, socialism will also have to reform society. We must work with community leaders to build a mass assembly of people in order to bring about the necessary change and reform the capitalist society of today. This can be done by fighting for causes that are close to you, either in your heart or geographically. You can also be a part of this change by joining your local protest group, trade union or political party. Solidarity is the first and most vital step.

By joining a party – or group – and talking to people about voting, you are making a small change to a system that runs on people's need to work and consume. Don't feel that your efforts are in vain.

They are not. If we don't change this system, then it will kill the planet and take us with it. We cannot allow this to happen.

Socialism must fight capitalism in government and in the community. Only then will it prevail and make a better, more equal world for all.

I hope you've enjoyed this brain spill of a book. You don't have to be a sandal-wearing hippy after reading it, but do consider voting for or joining your local socialist party. The great thing about this is that you can get involved as much or as little as you like.

The Left and socialists have always been the voice of the people and the visionaries in terms of how we can improve the future for everyone. The far right is trying to take this message and use it to spread their nationalistic and racist views. They claim to be against the system, but they support it and have no ideas about how to improve or reform the capitalist society we live in.

In recent years, the Left started to lose its way. But socialism is sexy again, and we are now able to fight back and take society with us – in the right direction. So we need to define what we believe in and what we stand for. We need to stand in solidarity with other workers and minorities and hold the system and the establishment elite to account. We can build a future that works for all. I hope this book goes some way towards achieving that.

Let me end by reminding you of how the book began: socialism is the language of change and offers a message of hope. Don't let that hope fade away. You may lose your faith in politics or even your country, but socialism is bigger than either of those things. It is what will help us build a better future: a future for the many, not the few.

Reading List
Please consider the following books

Socialism: A Very Short Introduction
by Michael Newman

Marx: A Very Short Introduction
by Peter Singer

Economics for the Many
by John McDonnell

For the Many: Preparing Labour for Power
by Mike Phipps

Why I'm No Longer Talking to White People About Race
by Reni Eddo-Lodge

Why Women Have Better Sex Under Socialism: And Other Arguments for Economic Independence
by Kristen R. Ghodsee

Inventing the Future Postcapitalism and a World Without Work
by Nick Srnicek and Alex Williams

Natives: Race and Class in the Ruins of Empire
by Akala

The Candidate: Jeremy Corbyn's Improbable Path to Power
by Alex Nunns

My Personal Favourite

The Lion and the Unicorn: Socialism and the English Genius by George Orwell

Bibliography

[1 K. Marx and F. Engles, The Communist Manifesto,
] London, 1848.

[2 K. Marx and F. Engels, The Communist Manifesto,
] London: Communist League, 1848.

[3 The Guardian, "Rana Plaza collapse: 38 charged with
] murder over garment factory disaster," *The Guardian,* 18
July 2016.

[4 Oxfam, "oxfam.org," January 2017. [Online]. Available:
] https://www.oxfam.org/sites/www.oxfam.org/files/file_a
ttachments/bp-economy-for-99-percent-160117-en.pdf.
[Accessed 2019].

[5] R. G. Wilkinson and K. Pickett, The Spirit Level: Why greater equality makes societies stronger., New York: Bloomsbury Press, 2009.

[6] R. G. Wilkinson and K. Pickett, The Inner Level : How More Equal Societies Reduce Stress, Restore Sanity and Improve Everyone's Wellbeing, London: Penguin Books Ltd, 2018.

[7] E. Feser, The Cambridge Companion to Hayek, Cambridge: Cambridge University Press, 2006.

[8] N. Klein, The Shock Doctrine: The Rise of Disaster Capitalism, New York : Picador, 2008.

[9] The Sutton Trust, "Leading People 2016," 2016. [Online]. Available: https://www.suttontrust.com/research-paper/leading-people-2016-education-background/. [Accessed 2019].

[10] M. Newman, Socialism: A Very Short Introduction, Oxford: Oxford University Press, 2005.

[11] N. McNaughton, Edexcel UK Government and Politics for AS/A Level Fifth Edition, London: Hodder Education , 2017.

[12] P. Singer, Marx: A Very Short Introduction, Oxford: Oxford University Press, 2018.

[13] D. Pegg, "The tech giants will never pay their fair share of taxes – unless we make them," *The Guardian,* 11 December 2017.

[14] Link Year and A. Donyes, "You Tube," October 2017. [Online]. Available: https://www.youtube.com/watch?v=vwx5IvypC5Q&t=2s.

[15] K. Noble, "How poverty affects children's brains," *Washington Post,* 2 October 2015.

[16] R. Eddo-Lodge, Why I'm No Longer Talking to White People About Race, New York: Bloomsbury Publishing, 2017.

[17] K. R. Ghodsee, Why Women Have Better Sex Under Socialism and Other Arguements for Economic Independence, London: Bodley Head, 2018.

[18] B. Bryson, Neither Here nor There: Travels in Europe, William Morrow & Co, 1992.

[19] C. Weller, "Dutch prisons are closing because the country is so safe," *The Independent,* 31 May 2017.

[20] D. Martin, "Labours botched PFI deals sent NHS costs soaring.," *The Daily Mail *freedom of Information sources,* 23 December 2013.

[21] G. Tetlow and J. Pickard, "Private companies make £831m profits from NHS contracts," *Financial Times,* 30 August 2017.

[22] NHS Support Federation, "Time to end the market experiment in the NHS? Contract report," December 2017. [Online]. Available: http://www.nhsforsale.info/uploads/images/contract%20 report%20dec%202017%2028_12_17%20.pdf.

[23] M. Scott Cato, "Virgin Care must be kept away from the NHS," *The Guardian,* 7 August 2018.

[24] ParlGov, "ParlGov," 2018. [Online]. Available: http://www.parlgov.org/explore/esp/party/902/.

[25] V. Wang, "https://www.nytimes.com/2018/06/27/nyregion/alexan dria-ocasio-cortez.html," *The New York Times,* 27 June 2018.

[2 Open Secrets, "New York District 14 2018 Race," 2018.

6] [Online]. Available:
https://www.opensecrets.org/races/summary?cycle=201
8&id=NY14.

[2 A. Rupar, "New Congress member creates stir by saying of
7] Trump: "We're going to impeach this motherfucker!"," 4
January 2019. [Online]. Available:
https://www.vox.com/policy-and-
politics/2019/1/4/18168157/rashida-tlaib-trump-
impeachment-motherfucker.

[2 C. Chappell, "Bernie Sanders' campaign said it raised a
8] whopping $5.9 million in first 24 hours," CNBC, 20 Feb
2019. [Online]. Available:
https://www.cnbc.com/2019/02/20/bernie-sanders-
campaign-said-it-raised-5-9-million-in-first-24-hours.html.

[2 Gallup, "Democrats More Positive About Socialism Than
9] Capitalism," 13 August 2018. [Online]. Available:
https://news.gallup.com/poll/240725/democrats-
positive-socialism-capitalism.aspx.

[3 A. Nunns, The Candidate, New York and London: OR
0] Books, 2018.

[3 BBC, "Labour leadership: Corbyn appeals for unity after
1] re-election," 24 September 2016. [Online]. Available:
https://www.bbc.com/news/uk-politics-37461219.

[3 Riley, Tess, "Just 100 companies responsible for 71% of
2] global emissions, study says," The Guardian, 20 July 2017.

[3 L. Elliot, "'This is about saving capitalism': the Dutch
3] historian who savaged Davos elite," The Guardian, 1
Febuary 2019.

[3 J. McDonnell and Various Authors, Economics for the
4] Many, London: Verso, 2018.

[3 N. Srnicek and A. Williams, Inventing the Future (revised

5] and updated edition): Postcapitalism and a World
Without Work, London: Verso, 2016.

[3 R. Bergman, Utopia for Realists: How We Can Build the
6] Ideal World, 2017: Little, Browen and Company, London.

[3 S. Fishwick, "How Karl Marx's legacy still lives on," *London*
7] *Evening Standard,* 9 May 2017.

[3 Wikipedia, "Spanish Socialist Workers' Party," January
8] 2019. [Online]. Available:
https://en.wikipedia.org/wiki/Spanish_Socialist_Workers
%27_Party.

Thanks for buying this book.

Keep an eye out for future books in this series

In Solidarity

Edward Lawrence

Made in the USA
San Bernardino, CA
22 May 2019